Dedicated to Laura,
my cohort in sibling revelry.

Jonah and the Whale... Shark?

Trilogy Christian Publishers
A Wholly Owned Subsidiary of Trinity Broadcasting Network
2442 Michelle Drive Tustin, CA 92780

Text and Illustration Copyright © 2022 by Charlie Williams
Character design by Calvin Williams, http://www.noiseguy.com

No part of this publication may be reproduced in whole or in part, or stored in a retrieval system, or transmitted in any form or by any means—electronic, mechanical, photocopying, recording, or otherwise—without written permission by the publisher and author. Printed in the USA. All rights reserved. Rights Department, 2442 Michelle Drive, Tustin, CA 92780.

The names, characters, places and incidents are products of the author's imagination and are used as literary references anyway. Any resemblance to actual locales or persons, living or dead or other, is entirely coincidental. The scanning, uploading, and distribution of this book without permission is a theft of the author's intellectual property. Thank you for your support of authors rights and the freedom of free expression in regards to parody. Parody is generally covered by the first amendment and in this instance it is meant as a comic rendering of an actual event, person, cultural reference or place.

SUMMARY: A hilarious but faithful retelling of Jonah's story. Jonah works for God but he doesn't like his new assignment. He runs in the opposite direction with his mascot Luke Worm. He weathers a storm, is swallowed by a big fish yet survives to inspire an entire Assyrian city. He learns that judgement should be left to the Lord. Based on biblical teaching, this is an anachronistic cartoon rendering. Jonah goes out of sync with God, he sinks, winds up in the drink. An artistic and anachronistic cartoon retelling of the Bible's book of Jonah.

For ages 7 and up, Grade level 3-7 and beyond. AR level 4.1.33.

For information about special discounts for bulk purchases, please contact Trilogy Christian Publishing.

Trilogy Disclaimer: The views and content expressed in this book are those of the author and may not necessarily reflect the views and doctrine of Trilogy Christian Publishing or the Trinity Broadcasting Network.

Manufactured in the United States of America
10 9 8 7 6 5 4 3 2 1
Library of Congress Cataloging-in-Publication Data is available.

ISBN: 978-1-68556-412-4
E-ISBN: 978-1-68556-413-1

JONAH AND THE WHALE... SHARK?

A long time ago, in a Galilee, far, far away...

Ha Ha, just kidding.

1. 2. 3. 4. 5. 6. 7.

...In modern day

Europe
Spain
Asia
Assyria
Galilee
Judah
Africa
Egypt

Israel,

1.

Shh!
CREEAK!
Hello? Honey? I'm home! Sorry I'm so late!
pet Rock
Tigga
tigga
tig

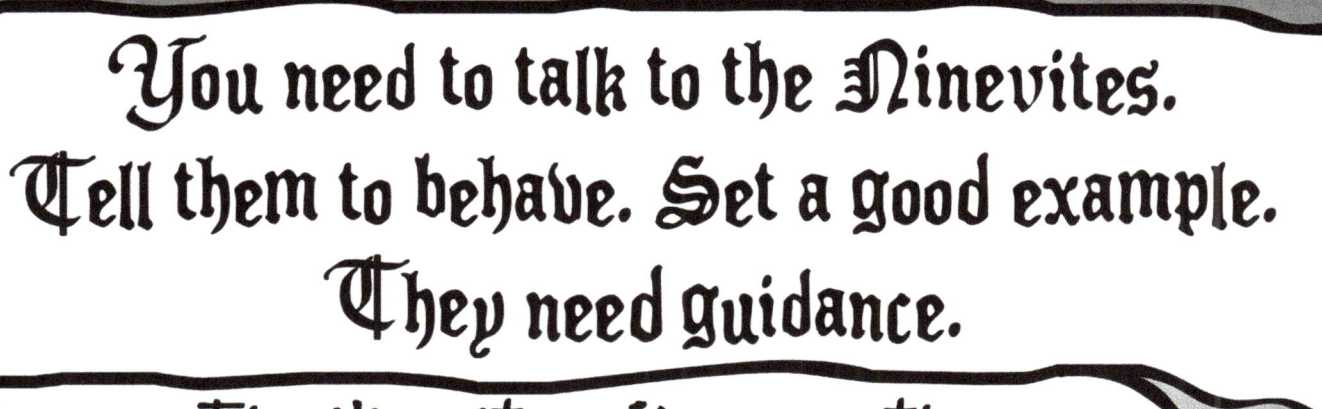

Hello! Sorry, I was in the shower.

Do what now? The Ninevites? Sure, I'll go talk to 'em.

Yeah, I'm listening. Yes. Uh-huh. Okay.

Ticka Tick

Even though I am claiming non-prophet status? Oh, okay. Yes, okay.

Sigh. Love You too. Bye-bye... bye-bye.

12

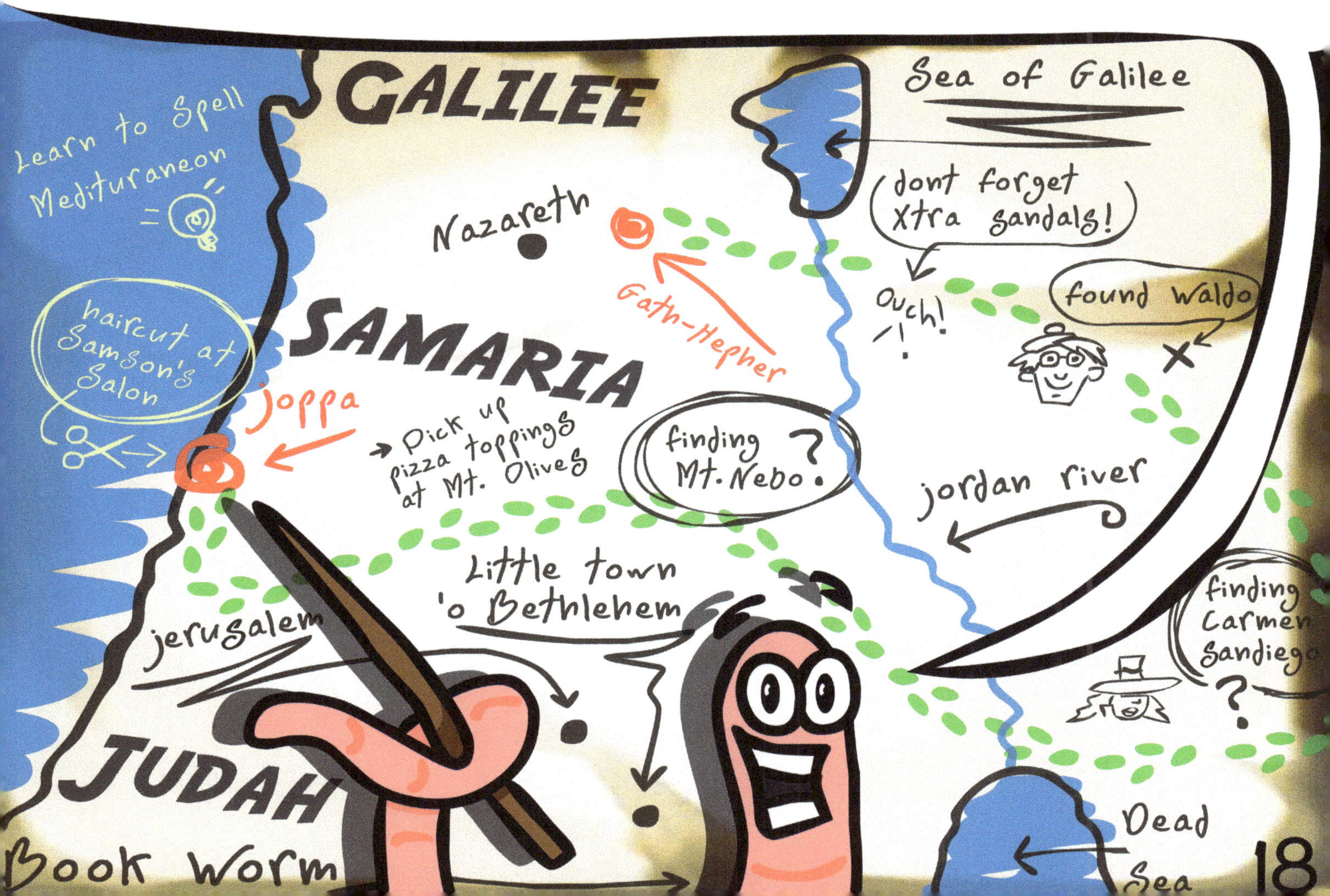

Luke Worm's Fun Facts!

Port of Joppa's trade route to Tarshish is 2,600 miles, one way. At 22 miles per hour, that takes 5 days.

TIDBITS

- When Jonah was a teenager, he was always borrowing the KEYS to go for a joyride... the donkeys.
- God's gifts surround you; that's why it's called "omnipresence."
- The Latin alphabet was created by the ancient Greeks! So yes, Greece IS the word.

THE FERTILE CRESCENT REFERS TO THE GREEN VALLEY THAT WAS NOT ALWAYS A **DESERT!** FROM THE DEAD SEA TO THE PERSIAN GULF, THE RIVERS WOULD **FLOOD** YEARLY, KEEPING THE CROPS GROWING.

Jonah and I had many adventures!
Here are two of his prophecies that came true:
King Jeroboam II expanded the borders of Israel.
The city of Lebo was restored.

Want to draw Jonah? It's easy!

1. Draw a bean shape for his head. Ha!
2. Draw two dots and a line.
3. Add hair and beard.
4. Doodle, it's free!

End of Chapter 1.

SPUH LASH!

Thank yooooo! Have a sunny day!

Pitooey

SO I'D LIKE TO KNOW WHERE, YOU GOT THE NOTION, TO ROCK THE BOAT, DON'T ROCK THAT BOAT BABY!

Ho boy. I'm in it now. Miles away from land!

Rock on with your bad self!

And that, dear reader, is when Jonah was swallowed by a whale...

SHARK?

End of Chapter 2.

GULP!

EEE-YUCK! That was worst water slide ever.
Okay, I was wrong, it CAN get worse.
So I'm in a whale shark's stomach. Good times.
This doesn't freak me out. Nooooo.

Whale means "large," and shark means I have a cartilage skellington like a shark. I'm a hybrid by name only.

Thank you, Ricky Peedia.

Oh, and technically, you aren't in my stomach, it's my maw. Thee? Pbthh. Pblth. Thorry, ith's hard to talk with my mouth full.

A MAW? What's that?

And where's your pa?

35

A *maw* is a mouth, throat, gullet, and stomach, all in one. Like the *crop* of a crow.

PRAWN

CHESS PRAWN

PLANKTON

KRILL

It's like having a drive-thru car wash in your body instead of chewing your food. Don't worry, I'm a filter feeder! I only eat plankton, krill and prawns.

Will you let us out, then?

Sorry, this is a one-way feed, and you won't fit out thru my gills. You're in there for good.

Now I know what a bagel feels like.

My name is Levi. Levi Athan.

36

That's a cool name. What's it mean?

I'm Jonah.

It's Hebrew for "dove."

Dove? Aww, cute. After what Noah sent out, huh?

Yeah, I'm like a bird, I'll only fly away.

Ha! Thank you, I needed a laugh. So, let me digest here. I have to eat a lot to maintain my size. GULP! BURP **I'm bigger than an 18-wheeler!**

SSSLURG

37

Normally I don't inhale humans, but it's WHALE SHARK WEEK! Thank you for choosing to be my meal. I'm not supposed to play with my food, so I guess I'll quit yammering now.

Dive, dive! Aaoogah!

Bloop!

Galoop!

Balubba lip!

JONAH SANK INTO THE DEPTHS OF THE SEA IN THE MAW OF A GIANT WHALE SHARK.

"I suppose there's some kinda lesson in all this, huh? **Fine.** So, pretty much, You're mad at me, right? I'm being punished, right? Okay, point taken! Don't mess with the Big Guy! Can I come out now? Hello? Aw, mannnn..."

Fun fact: exposition is a literary device that works anywhere.

Oh no, the salt water destroyed my cellphone!
I can't call for help!
I can't take a selfie!
I can't check my Fakebook page!
I can't see what everyone else is doing!
I can't see what people had for lunch on Insta-Grab!
I can't even play Candy Smush!
No screen time?
It's so quiet!

BLiP...
BLiP...

You're welcome.

End of Chapter 3.

Chapter 4. Reader's Digest.

PWEEE!

What are those?

Night vision goggles.

Why would a worm have night vision goggles?

Night bird-watching! I'm an owl spotter.

Sigh. Lord, I've been thinking. Things look pretty hopeless here. Inside a big smelly fish, at the bottom of the ocean for three days and nights... and on top of that, my wife is gonna kill me!

If she goes easy on you.

But I'm alive! Why? I'm ready to listen now. This blessing in disguise, Levi, was at the right place at the right time. I could've drowned or been eaten by a giant octopus or sumfin'. You saved me to do something important.

Peace 'a delivery.

I'm sorry I tried to run away from Your work. I can never get away from You... And now I know that is a good thing. I'm sorry. Will You forgive me?

Repent in da house, nice.

Uh... kinda like... how I should forgive... the Ninevites. I see the benefit of compassion.
Yeah. I get it. Do unto others as you'd want done to you.

Do unto others and déjà vu.

I read You loud and clear, over and out and Amen. P.S. Give me another chance?

From "Aww man" to "Amen."

42

GLEEM!

?

Whassat?

A text?

Yeah, right.

It says, "Hold your breath and hang on. LOL."

Selfie time!

#Godforgives #Survivethegulp

44

UGH, my dinner is not sitting right.

GRUMBLE

Whoa! How am I supposed to sit? Criss-cross applesauce? What's going on?

HERK! HAWK! HWACKK!

Now I know what a hairball feels like!

Slish!

45

SWASH·SWISH·SWOOSH
Ha-warf. Wharf!
Get a runnin' start...
ZOOM!
CCK! CCK!
Holdit-holdit-holdit...
HOCK, HAK!
SPITCHOOOOOOOO
GROSSSS!

SPIFF!

I'm glad to finally be out of that creature's mouth!

SLURP

Gaah!

DUDE... DID THAT WHALE OF A FISH... THING... JUST BARF YOU UP ONTO OUR BEACH?

Shore did.

Cool.

Where am I?

ASSYRIA, WHICH WILL BE SYRIA ONE DAY. NINEVEH IS JUST OVER THERE.

Munch munch

MWA HA HA
POW! POW!
CRASH
Rabble Rabble
SHRIEK!
RRRROC
OWIE!
ZZT ZZT
CRUNCH

Sounds dangerous.

47

Was someone fishing with you?
No, but my story IS miraculous.
Oh, we were bait all right. Hope we're off the hook?
JONAH TOLD THE PEOPLE WHAT HAPPENED AND HOW HE'D BEEN IN THE GULLET OF A WHALE SHARK.
HUH?
...THE BELLY OF A BIG FISH, FOR THREE DAYS.
This happened in the Mediterranean Sea? How'd you get all the way up the Tigris river?
The whale shark musta used a G.P.S.
HUH?
"God's Positioning System."
WHOA.

LEVI'S TRAVEL LOG!

Jonah's storm happened two days and 218 miles into his sea cruise. I swallowed him here. The storm moved east and flooded the Green Fertile Crescent. It was the worst storm in decades. One for the books!

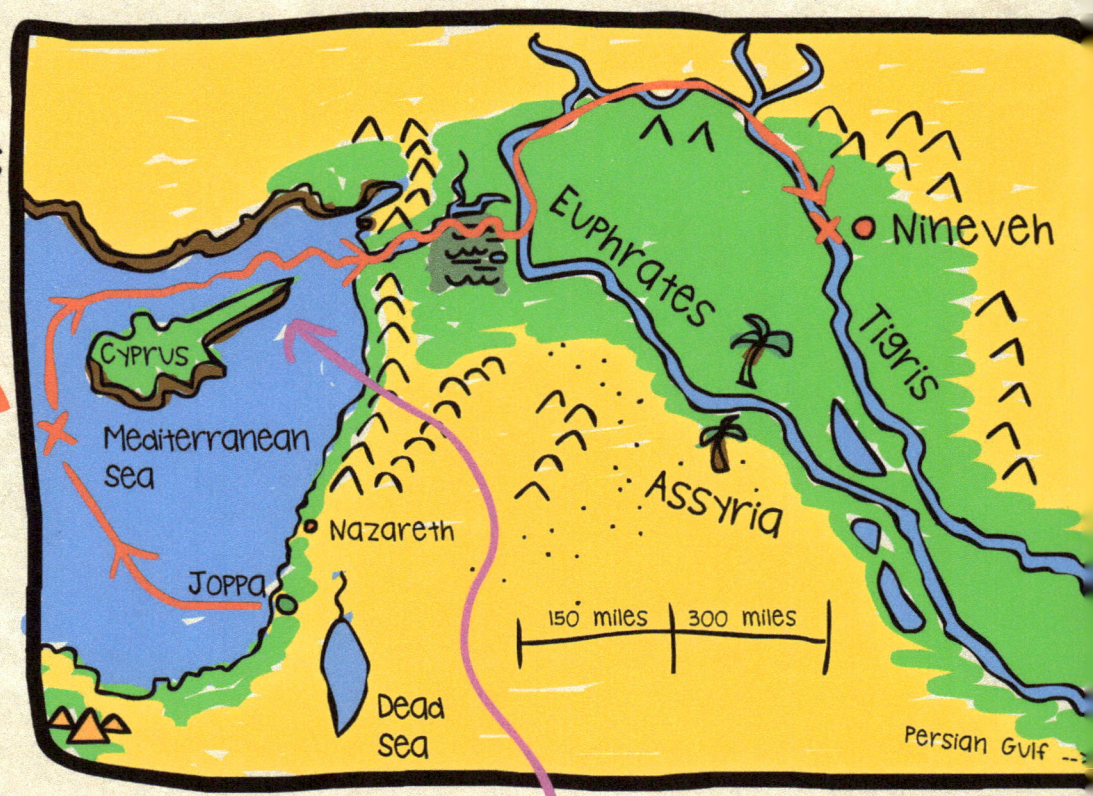

I am kind of near-sighted, but I saw a finger pointing the way! That island is called Cyprus. Can you see it too? I surfed the storm surge up the Orontes River. I know how to read the signs! I slipped across the flood plains and marshes into the Euphrates River and then into the Tigris River. It was all downstream from there.

ZOOM!

I normally only swim about 3 m.p.h. But with flowing flood waters, that added 6 m.p.h. to my speed. I was swimming at 9 miles per hour!

It's 430 miles across Assyria to Nineveh.

My trip was a total of 648 miles.

At 9 m.p.h. that took me 72 hours, which is three days

49

Nineveh!
In modern day Mosul, IRAQ.
Ancient Nineveh was the largest city in the world - at the time. It was the capital of the Assyrian empire from 1420-609 B.C.

Nineveh began as a fishing village around 6000 B.C. The name Nineveh means "a place of fish." The Assyrians built amazing structures using decorative architecture, making Nineveh a major trading post.

Map labels:
- Adad Gate
- Halahhu Gate
- Nergal Gate
- Shibaniba Gate
- Sin Gate
- Mushlalu Gate
- Zoo
- Ashurbanipal Palace
- Nabu Temple
- Khoser River
- Gate of watering places
- Ishtar Temple
- Library
- Botanical Gardens
- Kar-Mulissi Gate
- Quay Castle
- Palace of Sennacherib
- Quay Gate
- Desert Gate
- Shamash Gate
- Bouncy Castle
- Arsenal Gate
- Armory
- Halzi Gate
- Handuri Gate
- Tigris River
- 1 mile
- Ashur Gate

Assyrian Palaces

Nineveh also built a bad reputation and was soon feared as a cruel and ruthless city.

End of Chapter 4.

Chapter 5. Fall of Roam.

We're here LIVE at the main gate of Nineveh, where a man named Jonah is telling the Ninevites... an amazing story. Sources say God told him to come here to tell us all to "straighten up."

Ooooh!

I SMELL A RIOT! LOOK AT THIS MOB! BROADCAST THE CROWD'S REACTION TO THE WORLD

D PRESS

51

I ran away, was in a huge storm and sucked into the belly of a big fish. But I was saved by God, forgiven, redeemed, and then I was up-chucked onto your beach.
AMAZING!
MUNCH MUNCH
You tried to hide from the Creator but... He kept you alive and forgave you? That's so totally inspirational!
Forgiveness? Hmm... Let me look that up...
WHERE'S ALL THE RAGE AND VIOLENCE? GEEZ, LOOK AT THEM REPENT.
Repent? Hmm... "repent, verb: 1. to feel sorry for, regret one's past injustice."
"2. Decide to change one's life for the better."

THEY'RE ALL HUMBLE NOW. BOOOORING! LET'S GO.

I guess we gave Nineveh something to think about. Wow.

Let's go up the hill to get a good seat for the grand finale.

There's more? I thought this story was done!

Nuh-uh. Spoiler alert! It's time for His judgment. I did my part and told them about God's message. Now... we get to see His vengeance. Ack shun!

Snap Snap!

53

"Floods, volcanoes, earthquakes, or a monster meteor! Kuh-RASH! Pestilence, ya know? Angry locusts the size of mini-vans! Punishment! They don't deserve "forgiveness.""

"Lay off the energy drinks, Jojo!"

"Whew, it's hot. I'm burning up. Let's get under this tree that just suddenly bloomed. Thank you, Lord! The cool shade of that plump gourd."

Floof!

"What is a gourd?"

"A type of squash. Yummy!"

54

Now I guess I'll... Wha...? The gourd is shriveling up!

SKRITZZ

I'm full! BURP!

The worm?

PLORP!

What did you do?

Hello? What I always do! Eat! That squash had scrumptious roots!

55

YOU RUINED MY SHADE, YOU GLUTTONOUS WORM!

STOMP STOMP! STOMP!

SPROING

Yikes!

FWEEE

SPWOIT

You care more about that plant than the people of Nineveh!

Squiggle Scribble! Squirm

C'mon, Lord, help me out here! I just wanted to relax, and You let that worm gorge himself on MY gorgeous gourd.

Thlorp

56

Panel 1:
Jonah? You were happy just a minute ago. Do you enjoy being angry?

You spared the Ninevites but fried a gourd?

Panel 2:
Are you really mad about a plant withering? What is more important? Shade for your hot head, or a penitent people?

...

Yah, Yahweh!

Panel 3:
I see into people's hearts. You only see with your eyes. Leave the judgment to me.

Testify!

"Withering" is how fruits and vegetables produce seeds.
Kinda like how Jonah's story spreads seeds of understanding.
So what are you saying. I'm like the gourd?
Yes. You are out of your gourd.
Amen!
Oh, ha. Ha. God has a sense of humor.
Make a joyful noise!

If I can laugh, you can too. If I can forgive, so can you. The point of this story is repentance and forgiveness.

I see. Forgive me... again, for the second time in this story?

Forgiveness is unlimited.

I'm with You, Lord. Okay, let's get going! Wait till my wife hears about this!

Fwip!

Sorry about my hissy fit, Luke. We cool?

Yeah, but I'm hungry again.

bump

"Eww, I need a shower. Smells like I was in a fish for three days."

Sniff sniff!

Fip Fop

"Aroma de Jonah."

JONAH CAUGHT A BOAT DOWN THE TIGRIS RIVER TO THE PERSIAN GULF. HE SAILED AROUND SAUDI ARABIA AND UP THE RED SEA. HE PADDLED ALONG THE EGYPTIAN CANALS TO THE NILE RIVER, TO THE MEDITERRANEAN AND JOPPA.

Nineveh

500 miles

Mediterranean Sea

Joppa — "Cool!"

"Lovely gulf course."

Tigris River

Persian Gulf

Cairo canals

Jonah's return journey was a total of 5,350 miles - at 16 m.p.h., that's 17 days!

"Red? It's blue, actually."

Nile River

Red Sea

Saudi Arabia

"Longer, but quicker. If I walked, it would take me 70 days!"

Egypt

Indian Ocean

CREEEAK!
BLESS THIS MESS
Oh Judy, I'm baaack!

JONAH! YOU'VE BEEN GONE FOR A MONTH!

Naw, I was only gone four weeks.
WHERE WERE YOU? THIS'D BETTER BE GOOD.
Well, you're not going to believe this... uh... but... like... there was this big fish, err- I mean, whale shark and...
Tap tap

FWOOP

FUMP!

DINNER!

FLING

CRASH

NO CALLS, NO NUTHIN'! RUDE!

You got some 'splainin' to do.

63

DON'T COME IN UNTIL YOU CLEAN UP YOUR ACT!

Okay.

SHEEN!

Lord, have mercy!

Wink!

The End!

Slurrg

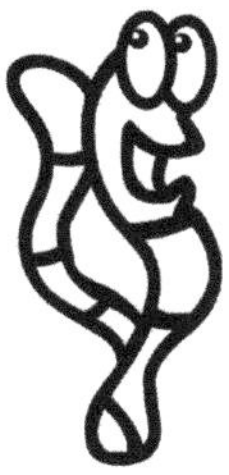

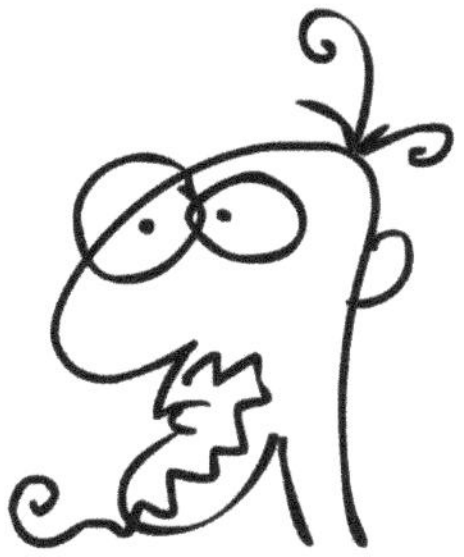

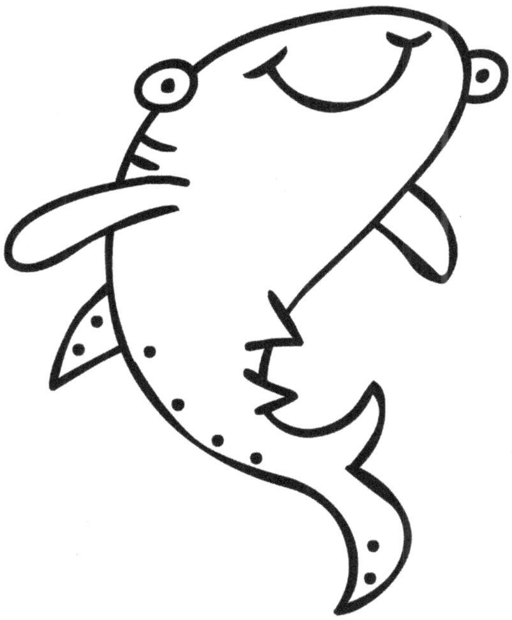

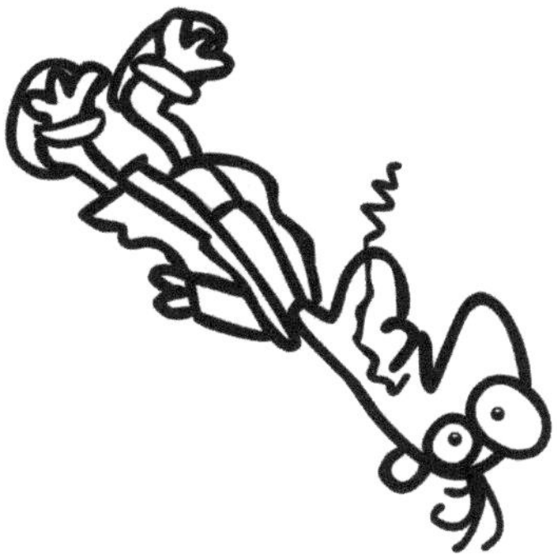

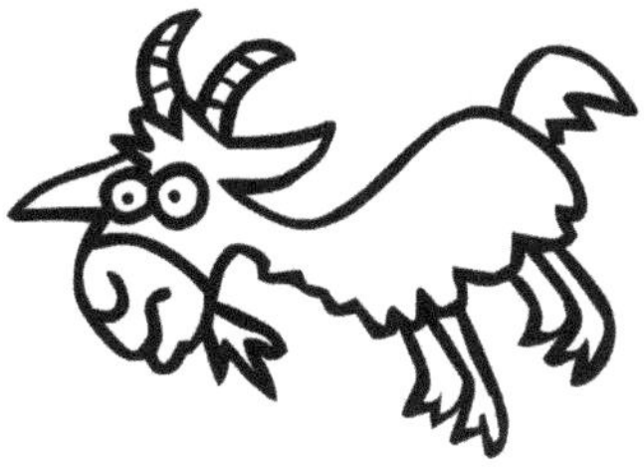

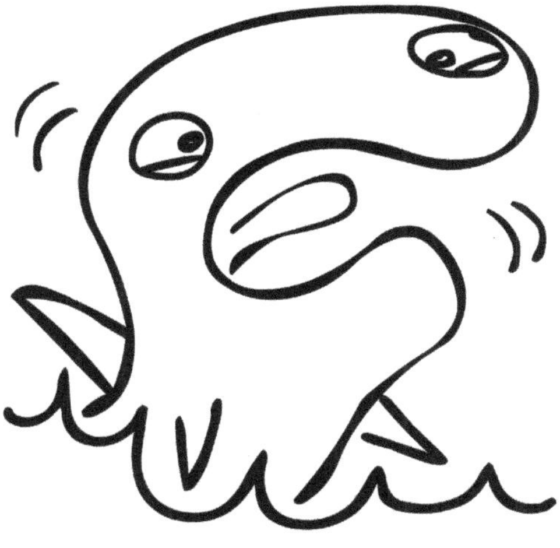

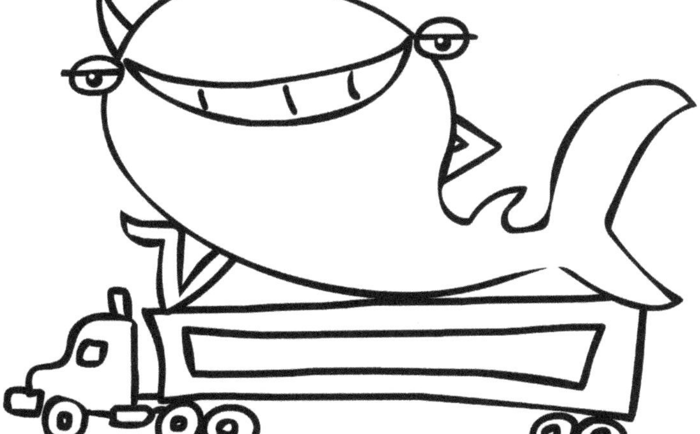

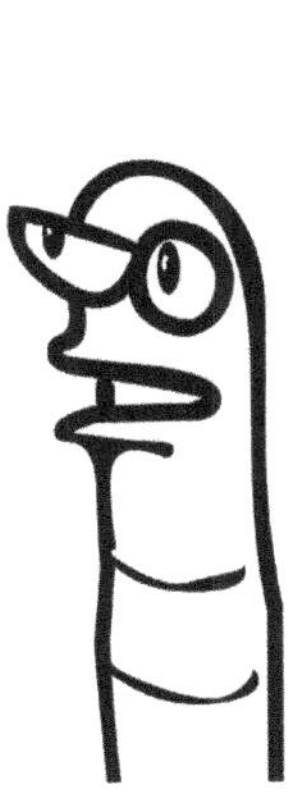

About the Author and Designer

Charlie and Calvin Williams are a father and son team of loony toonists.

Charlie has written many books for elementary and young adult readers. His first comics were created with his friends in 3rd grade. Later he published a daily comic strip called "Big Butte Junction" for the Daily Times in Wyoming. He has produced animated cartoons for WaterAid UK and ADRA Canada. He does great sound effect imitations and teaches readers the best way to use Onomatopoeia (..a vocal version of literary sounds in stories) during school and library visits across the U.S., Canada and Australia. During 2020-21, however, he was in the belly of a great big truck delivering toilet paper nationwide.

Calvin works in the field of cartoon animations, concept art and pre-visualization consultation. He animated "Dinosaurs in Cars" for a national musician and got to play a part in a library adventure video of "Sherlock Hounds" (with our basset hound, Monty).
   He says anyone can draw cartoons if they want and practice makes perfect. Keep on drawin'!

The Williams family lives in a state of constant wonder.

- Enjoy Jonah and the Whale... Shark? read by the author, complete with cartoons, animations, and sound imitations here: www.brigatoon.com

- Want to make a water noise with your mouth? Or learn a few other noises from this Jonah story, go to: www.brigatoon.com

- Watch our big floppy basset hound dressed as Sherlock, running in slow motion here: www.brigatoon.com

Be blessed and go with God!
Your pal,

Charlie Williams

CPSIA information can be obtained
at www.ICGtesting.com
Printed in the USA
JSHW010015200522
26117JS00004B/9

9 781685 564124